Behind the Scenes with Coders

COMPUTER NETWORK ARCHITECT

Barbara M. Linde

PowerKiDS press.

New York

Published in 2018 by The Rosen Publishing Group, Inc.
29 East 21st Street, New York, NY 10010

First Edition

Editor: Melissa Raé Shofner
Book Design: Rachel Rising

Photo Credits: Cover, kudla/Shutterstock.com; Cover (background) bluebay/Shutterstock.com; pp. 1, 3–32 (background) Lukas RS/Shutterstock.com; pp. 5, 29 Monkey Business Images /Shutterstock.com;p. 6 Dukes/Shutterstock.com; p. 9 scyther5/Shutterstock.com; p. 11 Jacob Lund/ Shutterstock.com; p.13 wavebreakmedia/Shutterstock.com; p. 15 Rvector/Shutterstock.com; p. 17 GaudiLab/Shutterstock.com; p. 19 Kjetil Kobjornsrud/Shutterstock.com; p. 21 Mediaphotos/Shutterstock.com; p. 23 dotshock/Shutterstock.com; p. 25 Leonardo da/Shutterstock.com; p. 26 Rawpixel.com/Shutterstock.com; p. 27 robuart/Shutterstock.com; p. 30 3DDock/Shutterstock.com.

Library of Congress Cataloging-in-Publication Data
Names: Linde, Barbara M., author.
Title: Computer network architect / Barbara M. Linde.
Description: New York : PowerKids Press, [2018] | Series: Behind the scenes
  with coders | Includes bibliographical references and index.
Identifiers: LCCN 2017001574| ISBN 9781508155782 (pbk. book) | ISBN
  9781508155607 (6 pack) | ISBN 9781508155720 (library bound book)
Subjects: LCSH: Computer network architectures–Vocational guidance–Juvenile
  literature. | Electrical engineering–Vocational guidance–Juvenile
  literature.
Classification: LCC TK5105.52 .L56 2018 | DDC 004.6023–dc23
LC record available at https://lccn.loc.gov/2017001574

Manufactured in the United States of America

CPSIA Compliance Information: Batch #BS17PK: For Further Information contact Rosen Publishing, New York, New York at 1-800-237-9932

Contents

Computer Network Architect to the Rescue!

Have you ever sent a file from a computer in your classroom to a computer in another classroom? Have you used your smartphone or tablet at a restaurant or library? Have you used a bank card to withdraw money from an ATM? You may have bought items from an online store. Surely you've surfed the net! If you've done any of these things, then you may have used the work of a computer **network** architect.

Computer network architects design and build computer and information networks. These networks might be for schools, businesses, or the government. Sometimes an individual has several computers that need to be networked. How does a computer network architect design a network? Read on to find out more about this fascinating career!

These students and their teacher are busily working on their tablets. Thanks to the work of a computer network architect, they can share information.

Networks All Around You

It's almost certain that you use some type of computer, if not every day, then at least a few times a week. A person can hardly live without one today! We e-mail, blog, chat, and send text messages. We shop and pay bills online. Businesses hold online meetings with people in different places—even different countries!

This image shows how several computers are connected in a network.

What's in a Network?

A network is made up of one or more computers with additional network devices. These devices are called **peripherals**. Printers, scanners, and webcams are types of network devices. Some networks are connected with wires that plug into the devices. Wireless networks are connected with radio waves. All the computers and other devices within a network are able to "talk" to one another. The information they share is called data.

When you use a computer to communicate with another computer or several computers, you become part of a network. In order for this network to operate properly, someone has to design its structure. This structure is often referred to as "architecture." In the field of construction, an architect designs and draws plans for buildings. In the field of computing, a network architect designs and draws plans for computer networks.

Location, Location, Location

Companies of all sizes need computer network architects. These businesses include banks, insurance companies, and telephone companies. Schools, hospitals, and government agencies use computer network architects, too. In fact, just about any place that uses computers needs a network architect.

A large company or school district may have several network architects on staff. A smaller company might have just one architect on staff. These people usually work full time, about 40 hours per week. Some companies are too small to have a full-time architect. Instead, they hire architects from a **consulting firm**. The firm sends an architect to do quick jobs now and then. Or this architect may work for the same small company for a few hours every month.

Tech Talk

A small group of computers in one building or in a few buildings close to each other is called a local area network, or LAN. Your school might use a LAN to connect computers in different classrooms. You may even have a small LAN in your home.

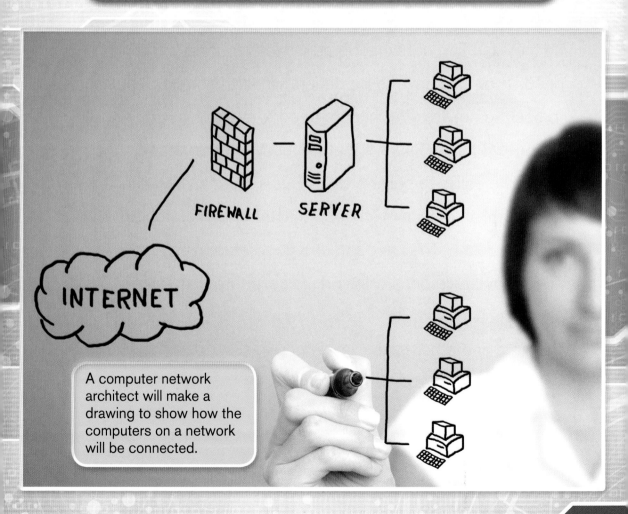

FIREWALL

SERVER

INTERNET

A computer network architect will make a drawing to show how the computers on a network will be connected.

It's Personal!

A computer network architect needs to be a "people person." Architects usually work with other computer specialists. They have to be able to manage others and work well in a group. They need to be careful listeners so they can find out what company leaders and workers need. They also have to be patient when they train people to use the network. Architects need to be able to explain **technical** things in ways that are easy to understand.

The ability to solve problems is a must. When things go wrong, a cool, calm, collected manner is the architect's best approach. They need to use good reasoning about how their ideas will work. Excellent reading skills are necessary, too. Architects read a lot of instruction booklets and other texts.

Tech Talk

A wide area network, or WAN, connects computers that are far away from each other. Do you send e-mails or have video chats with relatives in other states? You're using a WAN. The Internet is the largest WAN in the world!

A computer network architect interacts with many people while developing a plan for a network.

It's Technical!

A lot of thought and planning goes into creating a data communications network. A computer network architect thinks about questions such as: How many people will use this network? How many computers, printers, and other peripherals are needed? Where will the printers go? How many **servers** are needed to handle the workload? Where will the servers be located? What **software** is needed? How can we make sure the network stays secure?

Usually, the architect first creates a model of the network. The model includes the number and types of computers and peripherals. It shows where the servers will be located and how the wires will be connected. By studying the model, a computer network architect can figure out how a network will operate. Changes can be made even before the network is set up.

Network Protocols

A computer network uses a set of rules called protocols. You have rules in school that let you know when to talk, listen, wait, work, and so on. Network protocols tell the parts of a network how to behave so everything works properly. Some network protocols tell the computers when to send and receive messages. Other protocols tell the computers what to do if there is an error in the network.

This computer network architect is working in the server room. What do you think she is thinking about?

Now It's a Network

After the plan and model are ready, the architect presents them to the company leaders. The architect explains the plan and answers questions.

Next, the architect helps to build the physical network. They pay close attention to the details and mark the places in the building where the cables go. They figure out where the servers, printers, and other equipment belong. Some architects work right in the server room, connecting the wires and cables in the correct order. Other times, they give their plans to others who build the network. Of course, the computer network architect directs the work to make sure it's done correctly.

A network architect works behind the scenes much of the time. When things are running smoothly, network users don't even know the architect is there.

Tools of the Trade

Network **hardware** includes the devices you can see. The server is a computer that handles the information that goes to and from the other computers in the network. A modem lets computers communicate over the Internet. A router allows computers to join the same network. Cables connect computers and sometimes devices. Software isn't seen. It's the programs that run on the hardware. Software programs allow the network to operate and to complete specific tasks.

monitor

router

mouse

cable

computer tower

What Comes Next?

Information technology, or IT, changes all the time—and it changes very quickly! Computer network architects need to be one step ahead of the crowd. They spend a lot of time in meetings with company leaders. They may ask: Where is the company going? What new products might be added? How many workers will there be in three, five, or ten years? How much more data will be coming in and going out?

Computer network architects study the answers to these questions carefully. They try to guess what a company's future needs may be and develop a model that will fit these needs. They test hardware and software to see what will be most helpful. They may ask other architects for advice about their model. They also read books, papers, and websites to learn new information about the computer industry.

The Network Professional Association [NPA]

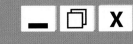

The NPA was created in 1991. Computer professionals from all over the world belong to this group. Its main purpose is to help members grow as professionals. Local chapter meetings give members a chance to meet with each other. The NPA reaches out to area students as well. Sometimes the NPA partners with other groups and businesses to put on professional and public events. Members read the group's online journal to stay current and publish articles to share their knowledge.

Computer network architects often work with a team of other computer professionals.

Network Maintenance

Computer network architects need strong skills to **analyze** the problem if part of a network breaks down. They diagnose, or figure out what went wrong, with the network. Then the architect decides how to fix the problem. The architect will either personally fix the network or give directions to **engineers** and repair people.

Networks have to be maintained, or kept in good working order. Each part of a network needs to be tested, and some parts may need to be replaced. Old hardware needs to be removed so new pieces can be put in. Software programs need updating. A computer network architect reads a lot about new hardware and software. They might take courses or go to conferences and other meetings to stay current.

Cybersecurity

Security is a big issue in computer networks. Computer network architects work with other IT people to keep hardware, software, and data safe. Some attacks can be prevented. For example, workers often need security badges to go into the rooms that contain the servers. Computer users need to log on with passwords. To protect data, architects construct firewalls. Firewalls are hardware or software that protect private data from unauthorized people outside a network.

This computer network architect is replacing a broken hard drive.

Education

To become a computer network architect, you'll need at least a bachelor's degree from a college or university. This degree usually takes four years to earn. It should be in computer science or information systems. It may also be in computer engineering or management information systems (MIS). Many companies also want a candidate to have a master's degree in **business administration** (MBA). This degree takes about one to two years of full-time study in addition to a bachelor's degree. Some people get a master of science degree in computer networking.

Software companies offer **certifications** related to their products. While these extra classes aren't required, they're quite helpful. Computer network architects never stop studying and learning. They keep up with all of the new products, machines, and methods.

These college students are taking a computer class. Some of them may graduate and become computer network architects.

Internships and Co-Ops

Internships and co-op jobs are good ways to see if a student and a job are a good fit. They're great for students hoping to work with computers someday. They may offer a foot in the door to a company. They also look great on a résumé. Some high schools and many colleges require students to take part in an internship. In some cases, a student volunteers, or works for free. In other cases, the student gets paid. Internships are usually part time during the school year, but they may be full time in the summer.

Co-op students work full time for a company for a time instead of going to school. The student gets paid for their work, which can last up to a year. Co-op students receive more detailed training and work experience because of this longer period of time.

Mentors Are Important!

A mentor is an experienced person working in your field. A mentor helps their mentee (the student or new worker) learn about the job and the company. A mentor might suggest college courses to take. Sometimes, the mentee works alongside the mentor. Other times, they simply meet and talk. A mentor can introduce the mentee to other important people in their field. The mentor/mentee relationship can last for many years—even for the course of an entire career!

Students gain valuable hands-on experience during internships and co-op jobs.

On the Way Up

Don't expect to get a computer network architect job right out of school. There are several other jobs you need to gain experience from when starting out on your career path. In fact, you'll probably spend between five and ten years doing other computer jobs first. The following jobs use skills that will help you grow into the job of a computer network architect:

- **A database administrator uses special software to keep track of all of the data for a company.**

- **An information security analyst focuses on keeping networks safe from cyberattacks.**

- **A support specialist helps workers learn to use the company's hardware and software.**

- **A hardware engineer works with circuit boards, routers, memory chips, and other hardware.**

- **A software developer creates new programs.**

- **A programmer writes and tests code.**

Knowing how to properly assemble the parts of a computer is an important skill for computer network architects.

Earning a Living

A salary is the amount of money you earn for a job. Computer network architects earn a high salary. According to government records for 2015, the median pay for this job was $100,240 per year. That's $48.19 per hour for a 40-hour workweek.

Computer network architects are needed to help design cloud-based networks. The "cloud" is a large network of servers where data may be stored, accessed, and shared.

The amount of money a computer network architect makes partly depends on where they work. Right now, some of the highest-paying jobs are in Washington, D.C., Boston, and New York City. Salary changes with experience, too. Entry-level workers might earn around $90,000 a year. Someone with 10 or more years of experience may make up to $123,000 a year. This job often has bonuses, or extra pay, for excellent work. There might be a bonus for finding a way to make a network safer or faster.

Start Now!

It's never too early to start preparing for a job. In school, take math, science, and computer classes, and don't forget about English. Excellent communication skills will help you work well with others. Well-written memos and letters make you look more professional. If there's a computer club at your school, you should join it. If there isn't one, talk to a teacher about getting one started. You may also be able to take computer classes at your local library or community center. Many colleges and universities have weekend programs for elementary, middle, and high school students, too.

Ask your teachers, parents, and other trusted adults if they know anyone who is working in the field. Perhaps you could shadow them on the job or work with them on simple projects.

Adults and kids can help each other use technology.

The Road Ahead

Computer network architects can look forward to a bright future. Experts say this field will keep growing, and the salary will keep increasing, too. Doctors and hospitals are going digital with patient records. More companies are switching to wireless networks. People are also starting to store more information in the cloud. Each of these types of IT needs someone to build its network. That person could be you!

Right now, there are more jobs for computer network architects than qualified people to fill them. Getting enough education and experience to work in this field takes a lot of hard work. If you're willing to put in the time, you'll have employers knocking at your door.

Glossary

analyze: To study something deeply.

business administration: A program of studies in a college that teaches students how to run a business.

certification: Proof that you know how to do something.

consulting firm: A company of experts that provides professional advice to an organization for a fee.

engineer: Someone who plans and builds machines.

hardware: The physical parts of a computer system, such as wires, hard drives, keyboards, and monitors.

internship: A job done—often without pay—in order to gain experience.

network: A system of computers and databases that are all connected. Also, to set up a system of computers and databases.

peripheral: A device connected to a computer to provide communication or other functions.

server: A computer or group of computers used by organizations for storing, processing, and distributing large amounts of data.

software: Programs that run on computers and perform certain functions.

technical: Of or relating to a mechanical or scientific subject.

Index

Websites

Due to the changing nature of Internet links, PowerKids Press has developed an online list of websites related to the subject of this book. This site is updated regularly. Please use this link to access the list: www.powerkidslinks.com/bsc/cna